A Purrfect Collection of Cat Quotes

By Sarah S. Davis

Legal

A Purrfect Collection of Cat Quotes by Sarah S. Davis

© 2019 Sarah S. Davis

All rights reserved. No portion of this book may be reproduced in any form without permission from the publisher, except as permitted by U.S. copyright law.

Cover by Sarah S. Davis

Image credits

Chapters 1, 2, 3, 4, 5 – Public domain via Pixabay

Table of Contents

DEDICATION

CHAPTER 1: THE WONDER OF WHISKERS   1

CHAPTER 2: PAWS AND PERSONALITY   12

CHAPTER 3: LIVING WITH LITTLE LIONS   28

CHAPTER 4: THE TAO OF THE TAIL   53

CHAPTER 5: FUNNY FELINES   71

ACKNOWLEDGMENTS   89

ABOUT THE AUTHOR   90

Dedication

To Bagheera, gone but never forgotten. I hope you're chasing mice in heaven.

Chapter 1: The Wonder of Whiskers

The Majesty of Cats

Cats are stunning creatures of rare beauty. Each cat we meet evokes a sense of wonder. In this chapter, we celebrate cat magic.

"If there were to be a universal sound depicting peace, I would surely vote for the purr." — Barbara L. Diamond

"A cat is only technically an animal, being divine." — Robert Lynd

"Respecting a cat is the beginning of the aesthetic sense." — Erasmus Darwin

"Cats are a mysterious kind of folk." — Sir Walter Scott

"A kitten is, in the animal world, what a rosebud is in the garden." — Robert Sowthey

"I think that cats are spirits incarnated on Earth. A cat, I am sure, could walk on a cloud without falling through it." — Jules Verne

"Elegance wanted body and life, which is why it turned into a cat." — William IX, Duque of Aquitain

"Kittens are angels with whiskers." — Alexis Flora Hope

"The smallest feline is a masterpiece." — Leonardo da Vinci

"It always gives me a shiver when I see a cat seeing what I can't see." — Eleanor Farjeon

"Prowling his own quiet backyard or asleep by the fire, he is still only a whisker away from the wilds." — Jean Burden

"I think that the world should be full of cats and full of rain, that's all, just cats and rain, rain and cats, very nice, good night." — Charles Bukowski, *Betting on the Muse: Poems and Stories*

"If a fish is the movement of water embodied, given shape, then cat is a diagram and pattern of subtle air." — Doris Lessing, *On Cats*

"A cat's rage is beautiful, burning with pure cat flame, all its hair standing up and crackling blue sparks, eyes blazing and sputtering." — William S. Burroughs, *The Cat Inside*

"After dark, all cats are leopards." — Alison Davies, *Be More Cat*

"Another cat? Perhaps. For love there is also a season; its seeds must be resown. But a family cat is not replaceable like a worn-out coat or a set of tires. Each new kitten becomes its own cat, and none is repeated. I am four cats old, measuring out my life in friends that have succeeded but not replaced one another." — Irving Townsend

"Cats were weird." — Stephen King, *Pet Sematary*

"A cat can purr its way out of anything." — Donna McCrohan

"A house isn't a home without the ineffable contentment of a cat with its tail folded about its feet. A cat gives mystery, charm, suggestion." — L.M. Montgomery, *Emily's Quest*

"Cats are endless opportunities for revelation." — Leslie Kapp

"Two things are aesthetically perfect in the world—the clock and the cat." — Emile Auguste Chartier

"Indeed, there is nothing on this earth more peaceful than a sleeping, purring cat." — Jonathan Scott Payne, *Mighty Little Man*

"You cannot look at a sleeping cat and feel tense." — Jane Pauley

Cat Lover in Focus: *Colette* (1873-1954)

The trailblazing, bohemian French writer Colette was the original cat lady. Cats perfectly embodied Colette's fierce independent streak, unapologetic pursuit of pleasure, and boundless confidence.

"There are no ordinary cats." — Colette

Colette's bond with cats was well known, leading her second husband to remark: "When I enter a room where you're alone with animals, I feel I'm being indiscreet." Perhaps that jealousy is what inspired Colette's 1933 novel, *The Cat*. This book depicts the hopeless love heroine Camille feels for Alain. The problem? Alain worships his cat more than anyone.

"The cat is the animal to whom the creator gave the biggest eyes, the softest fur, the most supremely delicate nostrils, a mobile ear, an unrivaled paw, and a curved claw borrowed from the rose tree." — Colette

Chapter 2: Paws and Personality

Cattitude

We've all come across it...cat attitude, or "cattitude." One could never accuse a cat of not having a personality. These cute creatures have a reputation for doing things on their terms, living the life they want to live, and not groveling for attention from humans. In Chapter 2, we'll hear all about this notorious cattitude.

"A cat is nobody's fool." — Heywood Brown

"Curiosity killed the cat." — Ben Johnson

"In a cat's eye, all things belong to cats." — Unknown

"I would like to see anyone, prophet, king or God, convince a thousand cats to do the same thing at the same time." — Neil Gaiman

"If cats could talk, they wouldn't." — Nan Porter

"I am what I am. I would tell you what you want to know if I could, for you have been kind to me. But I am a cat, and no cat anywhere ever gave anyone a straight answer." — Peter S. Beagle, *The Last Unicorn*

"Dogs have their day, but cats have 365." — Lilian Jackson Braun

"Dogs come when they're called; cats take a message and get back to you later." — Mary Bly

"Sleep is like a cat. It only comes to you if you ignore it." — Gillian Flynn

"Cats are connoisseurs of comfort." — James Herriot

"Women and cats will do as they please, and men and dogs should relax and get used to the idea." — Robert Heinlein

"Witches were a bit like cats. They didn't much like one another's company, but they did like to know where all the other witches were, just in case they needed them." — Terry Pratchett, *A Hat Full of Sky*

"Cats randomly refuse to follow orders to prove they can." — Ilona Andrews, *Magic Strikes*

"Let us be honest: most of us rather like our cats to have a streak of wickedness. I should not feel quite easy in the company of any cat that walked around the house with a saintly expression." — Beverly Nichols, *Beverly Nichols' Cats' A-Z*

"I am not a cat man, but a dog man, and all felines can tell this at a glance—a sharp, vindictive glance." — James Thurber

"With my aversion to this cat, however, its partiality for myself seemed to increase." — Edgar Allan Poe, "The Black Cat"

"The mathematical probability of a common cat doing exactly as it pleases is the one scientific absolute in the world." — Lynn M. Osband

"Cats are absolute individuals, with their own ideas about everything, including the people they own." — John Dingman

"From birds she learned how to sing; from cats she learned a form of dangerous independence." — Salman Rushdie

"A dog is a dog, a bird is a bird, and a cat is a person." — Mugsy Peabody

"Cats are people, and the sooner the world accepts that fact, the better off the world will be." — H. Allen Smith, *Rhubarb*

"Never try to out-stubborn a cat." — Robert Heinlein

"Cats seem to go on the principle that it never does any harm to ask for what you want." — Joseph Wood Krutch

"The cat could very well be man's best friend but would never stoop to admitting it." — Doug Larson

"The cat is domestic only as far as suits its own needs." — Saki, "The Achievement of the Cat"

"Cats don't like change without their consent." — Roger A. Caras

"I am as vigilant as a cat to steal cream." — William Shakespeare, *Henry IV*

"In the middle of a world that has always been a bit mad, a cat walks with confidence." — Roseanne Amberson

"Cats invented self esteem. There is not an insecure bone in their body." — Erma Bombeck

"The reason cats climb is so that they can look down on almost any other animal….it's also the reason they hate birds." — KC Buffington

"One reason we admire cats is for their proficiency in one-upmanship. They always seem to come out on top, no matter what they are doing, or pretend they do." — Barbara Webster

"Cats always know whether people like or dislike them. They do not always care enough to do anything about it." — Winifred Carriere

"The great charm of cats is their rampant egotism, their devil-may-care attitude toward responsibility, their disinclination to earn an honest dollar." — Robertson Davies

"If I called her she would pretend not to hear but would come a few moments later when it could appear that she had thought of doing it first." — Arthur Weigall

"My cat is not insane; she's just a really good actress." — P.C. Cast, *Untamed*

"Anyone who claims that a cat cannot give a dirty look has either never kept a cat or is singularly unobservant." — Maurice Burton

"No one had ever accused Koko of being naughty. Perverse, perhaps, or arrogant, or despotic. But naughtiness was beneath his dignity." — Lilian Jackson Braun

Cat Lover in Focus: William S. Burroughs

Groundbreaking experimental American writer William S. Burroughs was a known cat lover. Burroughs wrote a book about cats, *The Cat Inside* (1986), praising their companionship and spunky personality. Burroughs subscribed to *Cat Fancy* magazine, and though he offered to write a story for them, the renegade Beat author was turned down.

Burroughs kept many cats at his house in Lawrence, Kansas. The cats were frequent fixtures in the town, each with its own personality.

Here's Burroughs with "Ginger":

"The cat does not offer services. The cat offers itself. Of course he wants care and shelter. You don't buy love for nothing." — William S. Burroughs, The Cat Inside

The final entry in Burroughs's journal is a testament to his lifelong love for cats. Reflecting on the concept of love, Burroughs writes:

Only thing can resolve conflict is love, like I felt for Fletch and Ruski, Spooner, and Calico. Pure love. What I feel for my cats present and past.
Love? What is it?
Most natural painkiller what there is.
LOVE.

When Burroughs died, he was laid to rest in his backyard among his "cat graveyard."

"Like all pure creatures, cats are practical." — William S. Burroughs

27

Chapter 3: Living with Little Lions

Our Relationship with Cats

While dogs are known as "man's best friend," cats have a reputation for being standoffish and remote. But anyone who lives with these little lions knows cats are capable of great affection and admiration—on their terms. Nothing feels better than the hard-won affection of a cat.

"Time spent with cats is never wasted." — Sigmund Freud

🐾

"Cats choose us: we don't own them." — Kristin Cast

🐾

"It is impossible to keep a straight face in the presence of one or more kittens." — Cynthia E. Varnado

🐾

"What greater gift than the love of a cat?" — Charles Dickens

🐾

"There are two means of refuges from the miseries of life: music and cats." — Albert Schweitzer

🐾

"A cat will be your friend, but never your slave." — Theophile Gautier

🐾

"As every cat owner knows, nobody owns a cat." — Ellen Perry Berkeley

🐾

"There are few things in life more heartwarming than to be welcomed by a cat." — Tay Hohoff

"I take care of my flowers and my cats. And enjoy food. And that's living." — Ursula Andress

"It is good to have a lot of cats around. If you feel bad, you look at the cats and you feel better, because they know that things are as they are." — Charles Bukowski

"God made the cat to offer men the pleasure of stroking a tiger." — Francois Joseph Mery

"Cats know instinctively the exact time their masters are going to wake up, and wake them ten minutes earlier." — Jim Davis

"Dogs look at us as their gods, horses as their peers, but the cats look to us as their subjects." — Winston Churchill

"Cats are good masters, as long as you remember what your own place is." — Paul Gray

"The cat is the only animal that has managed to tame man." — Marce Mauss

"You can't ever be a cat owner; in the best of cases it allows you to be their companion." — Harry Swanson

"How you behave toward cats here below determines your status in Heaven." — Robert Heinlein

"One cat just leads to another." — Ernest Hemingway

"Anyone who believes what a cat tells him deserves all he gets." — Neil Gaiman

"I have found it surprisingly difficult to remain sad when a cat is doing its level best to sandpaper one's cheeks." — R.L. LaFevers, *Theodosia and the Last Pharaoh*

"We need cats to need us. It unnerves us that they do not. However, if they do not need us, they nonetheless seem to love us." — Jeffrey Masson

"I realized that cats make a perfect audience, they don't laugh at you, they never contradict you, there's no need to impress them, and they won't divulge your secrets." — Elle Newmark, *The Book of Unholy Mischief*

"There are many intelligent beings in the Universe. Most of them are owned by cats." — Old Polish Proverb

"Sunday, January 27, 1884. -- There was another story in the paper a week or so since. A gentleman had a favourite cat whom he taught to sit at the dinner table where it behaved very well. He was in the habit of putting any scraps he left onto the cat's plate. One day puss did not take his place punctually, but presently appeared with two mice, one of which it placed on its master's plate, the other on its own." — Beatrix Potter, *Beatrix Potter's Journal*

🐾

"Can I Tinder swipe for cat cuddles?" — Shannon M. Mullen, *See What Flowers*

🐾

"Once [a cat] has given its love, what absolute confidence, what fidelity of affection! It will make itself the companion of your hours of work, of loneliness, or of sadness. It will lie the whole evening on your knee, purring and happy in your society, and leaving the company of

creatures of its own society to be with you." —
Théophile Gautier, *Ménagerie Intime*

"Ordinarily the death of a cat means little to most men, a lot to fewer men, but to me, and that cat, it was exactly and no lie and sincerely like the death of my little brother - I loved Tyke with all my heart." — Jack Kerouac, *Big Sur*

"Very early on, I understood that I secretly and mysteriously belonged to the world of cats." — Balthus, *Vanished Splendors: A Memoir*

"A cat can make you feel well rested when you're tired or turn a rage into a calm just by sitting on your lap. His very nearness is a healing song." — Shannon Hale, *Book of a Thousand Days*

"Once a cat loves you, it loves you till the end." — Will Advise

"Every cat knows how to keep his owner feeding them: You may scratch and bite ninety-nine times, but the hundredth time, you must leap into a lap and press your nose to their nose. Rules are for dogs." — Catherynne M. Valente, *The Girl Who Raced Fairyland All the Way Home*

"By associating with the cat, one only risks becoming richer." — Colette

"I think I would rather have a cat than a sweetheart, after all. They are less trouble, and even the handsomest sweetheart is sadly lacking in fur." — Laura Amy Schlitz, *The Hired Girl*

"A cat chooses its owner, not the other way around." — Helen Brown, *Cleo*

"A happy arrangement: many people prefer cats to other people, and many cats prefer people to other cats." — Mason Cooley

"The way to get on with a cat is to treat it as an equal—or even better, as the superior it knows itself to be." — Elizabeth Peters

"Authors like cats because they are such quiet, loveable, wise creatures, and cats like authors for the same reasons." — Robertson Davies

🐾

"Happy is the home with at least one cat." — Italian Proverb

🐾

"There is something about the presence of a cat that seems to take the bite out of being alone." — Louis J. Camuti

🐾

"When I play with my cat, who knows if I am not a pastime to her more than she is to me?" — Michel de Montaigne

🐾

"I was drawn to his aloofness, the way cats gravitate toward people who'd rather avoid them." — Rachel Hartman

"There should always be one more cat than person, so everyone has one to pet, and I have two to myself." — Jarod Kintz

"We need cats to need us. It unnerves us that they do not. However, if they do not need us, they nonetheless seem to love us." — Jeffrey Moussaieff Masson

"It is a truth universally acknowledged that a man in possession of a warm house and a well-stocked fridge must be in want of a cat." — Heather Hacking

"The amazing activity of the cat is delicately balanced by his capacity for relaxation. Every household should contain a cat, not only for decorative and domestic values, but because the cat in quiescence is medicinal to irritable, tense, tortured men and women." — William Lyon Phelps

"There is no known cure for severe affection for one's cat. The only way to relieve the symptoms is to go ahead and launch a kiss attack." — Tichakorn Khroopan Hil

"The human race can be roughly divided into two categories: ailurophiles and ailurophobes – cat lovers and the underprivileged." — David Taylor

"After all, a woman who doesn't love cats is never going to be make a man happy." — Orhan Pamuk

"...when I returned home at night, he was pretty sure to be waiting for me near the gate and would rise and saunter along the walk, as though his being there was purely accidental." — Charles Dudley Warner

"The trouble with sharing one's bed with cats is that they'd rather sleep on you than beside you." — Pam Brown

"Cats are designated friends." — Norman Corwin

"A cat allows you to sleep on the bed. On the edge." — Jenny de Vries

"In the beginning, God created man, but seeing him so feeble, He gave him the cat." — Warren Eckstein

"Every life should have nine cats." — Anonymous

"You will always be lucky if you know how to make friends with strange cats." — Colonial American Proverb

"Cats come and go without ever leaving." — Martha Curtis

Cat Lover in Focus: Edward Gorey

American artist, writer, and illustrator Edward Gorey left behind a reputation for his dark sense of humor, his macabre imagination, and his love of cats. In many of his drawings and books for children, Gorey incorporates feline elements.

Gorey told *Vanity Fair* that cats were the greatest love of his life and said that if he could change one thing about his family, it would be: "To live with cats who are a tad less loopy."

One of the most famous cat-themed collaborations was between acclaimed Modernist poet T.S. Eliot and Edward Gorey. In Eliot's *Old Possum's Book of Practical Cats* (1939), the normally serious author gives into whimsy in his poetry about quirky cat characters.

Gorey provided illustrations that brought the cats to life with a 1982 edition, like in the illustration above.

The book was later adapted into the Broadway musical, *Cats*.

Gorey was, like many creative types, a bit of a recluse. He surrounded himself with cats and loved their company. Cats are definitely great companions to keep even the most introverted person connected to others.

"I talk to my cats a lot now," he told *People* magazine. "That prevents me from talking to myself."

When Gorey died in 2000, part of his ashes were saved to be buried with two of his favorite cats upon their future death.

He is often remembered for his quote:
"Books. Cats. Life is good."

Chapter 4: The Tao of the Tail

Cat Wisdom

Cats are wise creatures. They have much to teach us. In this chapter, we celebrate the lessons we learn from our feline companions.

"A cat has beauty without vanity, strength without insolence, courage without ferocity, all the virtues of man without his vices." — Lord Byron

"Way down deep, we're all motivated by the same urges. Cats have the courage to live by them." — Jim Davis

"A cat has absolute emotional honesty. Human beings, for one reason or another, may hide their feelings, but a cat does not." — Ernest Hemingway

"Cats know how to obtain food without labor, shelter without confinement, and love without penalties." — W.L. George

"The animal that the Egyptians worshiped as divine and the Romans worshiped as a symbol of freedom, has shown in all ages two closely linked characteristics: courage and self-respect." — Dave Barry

"The ideal of calm exists in a sitting cat." — Jules Renard

"You cannot live with a paw in each world." — Erin Hunter, *Into the Wild*

"I have lived with several Zen masters—all of them cats." — Eckhart Tolle, *The Power of Now*

"I have studied many philosophers and many cats. The wisdom of cats is infinitely superior."
— Hippolyte A. Taine

"I'm a cat. We aren't required to make sense."
— Seanan McGuire, *A Local Habitation*

"What sort of philosophers are we, who know absolutely nothing of the origin and destiny of cats?" — Henry David Thoreau

"All cat stories start with this statement: 'My mother, who was the first cat, told me this...'"
— Shirley Jackson, *We Have Always Lived in the Castle*

"For, though the room was silent, the silence of half a hundred cats is a peculiar thing, like fifty individual silences all piled on top of another."
— Susanna Clarke, *Jonathan Strange & Mr Norrell*

"Human beings are drawn to cats because they are all we are not—self-contained, elegant in everything they do, relaxed, assured, glad of company, yet still possessing secret lives." — Pam Brown

"Cats tell me without effort all there is to know." — Charles Bukowski, *On Cats*

"When a cat flatters ... he is not insincere: you may safely take it for real kindness." — Walter Savage Landor

"Cats liked to occupy liminal spaces: both inside and outside, both tame and wild, both yawn and meow." — Gail Carriger, *Competence*

"Curled up on one of her pillows a gray fluff of kitten yawned, showing its pink tongue, tucked its head under again, and went back to sleep." — Madeline L'Engle, *A Wrinkle in Time*

"Everyone has noticed the taste which cats have for pausing and lounging between the two leaves of a half-shut door. Who is there who has not said to a cat, 'Do come in!' There are men who, when an incident stands half-open before them, have the same tendency to halt in indecision between two resolutions, at the risk of getting crushed through the abrupt closing of the adventure by fate. The over-prudent, cats as they are, and because they are cats, sometimes incur more danger than the audacious." — Victor Hugo, *Les Misérables*

"Cats will be cats." — Morrissey, *Autobiography*

"Cats aren't special advisers. They advise us all the time, whether we want them to or no."— Tamora Pierce, *Wolf-Speaker*

"Purr more, hiss less." — Linda C. Marchman

"I love cats because I enjoy my home, and, little by little, they become its visible soul." — Jean Cocteau

"Cats are intended to teach us that not everything in nature has a function." — Garrison Keillor

"Cats are at home everywhere where one feeds them." — German Proverb

"All cats love fish but fear to wet their paws." — Chinese Proverb

🐾

"One reason that cats are happier than people is that they have no newspapers." — Gwendolyn Brooks

🐾

"I've found that he way a person feels about cats-and the way they feel about him or her in return-is usually an excellent gauge by which to measure a person's character." — P.C. Cast

🐾

"When the mouse laughs at the cat, there's a hole nearby." — Nigerian Proverb

"Cats are only human. They have their faults." — Kingsley Amis

"With the qualities of cleanliness, discretion, affection, patience, dignity, and courage that cats have, how many of us, I ask you, would be capable of being cats?" — Fernand Mery

"There is, indeed, no single quality of the cat that man could not emulate to his advantage."
— Carl Van Vechten

"There are many intelligent creatures in the universe and they are all owned by cats." — Anonymous

"No tame animal has lost less of its native dignity or maintained more of its ancient reserve. The domestic cat might rebel tomorrow." — William Conway

"Cats are inquisitive, but hate to admit it." — Mason Cooley

"A cat is never vulgar." — Carl Van Vechten

"Cats must have three names—an every day name, such as Peter; a more particular, dignified name, such as Quaxo, Bombalurina, or Jellylorum; and, thirdly, the name the cat thinks up for himself, his deep and inscrutable singular Name." — T.S. Eliot

"A cat's got her own opinion of human beings. She don't say much, but you can tell enough to make you anxious not to hear the whole of it."
— Jerome K. Jerome

"There is no more intrepid explorer than a kitten." – Jules Champfleury

"A cat is a puzzle for which there is no solution."
— Hazel Nicholson

Cat Lover in Focus: Freddie Mercury

Queen singer Freddie Mercury was the ultimate cat dad. Mercury was incredibly affectionate with his cats and would often call home while on tour and ask to speak to them. Mercury's former lover and lifelong friend Mary Austin would put the phone to the cats so Mercury could check in on his brood.

Mercury's cats roamed freely around his mansion, with as many as ten kitties at a time prowling the palace. According to *The Telegraph*, Mercury often rescued cats from the Blue Cross shelter in London. Among these were Miko, Romeo, Lily, and Goliath.

In the last record the band recorded, *Innuendo*, Mercury wrote a song about Delilah, one of his favorite felines. Delilah was a bewitching tabby that Mercury adopted in 1987.

Mercury made his views known on being a cat lover in the liner notes to his solo album, Mr. Bad Guy. Mercury dedicated the notes to Jerry, one of his cats, adding:

"This album is dedicated to my cat Jerry—also Tom, Oscar, and Tiffany and all the cat lovers across the universe—screw everybody else!"

Chapter 5: Funny Felines

Cat Humor

Cats have a curious sense of humor. Contrary to popular belief, they are one of the most playful pets, often playing tricks on each other, sleeping in improbable and ridiculous positions, and making their humans laugh. Collected here are quotes that capture the funny side of felines.

"In ancient times, cats were worshipped as gods; they have not forgotten this." — Terry Pratchett

"Cats have it all: admiration, an endless sleep, and company only when they want it." — Rod McKuen

"A lie is like a cat: you need to stop it before it gets out the door or it's really hard to catch." — Charles M. Blow

"The only thing a cat worries about is what's happening right now. As we tell the kittens, you can only wash one paw at a time." — Lloyd Alexander, *Time Cat*

"If cats could write history, their history would mostly be about cats." — Eugene Weber

"To err is human, to purr is feline." — Robert Byrne

"The problem with cats is that they get the same exact look whether they see a moth or an axe-murderer." — Paula Poundstone

"People who don't like cats were probably mice in an earlier life." — Unknown

"When Rome burned, the emperor's cats still expected to be fed on time." — Seanan McGuire

"In my head, the sky is blue, the grass is green and cats are orange." — Jim Davis, *In Dog Years I'd be Dead: Garfield at 25*

"I wish that my writing was as mysterious as a cat." — Edgar Allan Poe

"If I prefer cats to dogs it is because there are no police cats." — Jean Cocteau

"The phrase 'domestic cat' is an oxymoron." — George Will

"Cats gravitate to kitchens like rocks gravitate to gravity." — Terry Pratchett

"Cats can work out mathematically the exact place to sit that will cause most inconvenience."
— Pam Brown

"'Meow' means 'woof' in cat." — George Carlin

"I am fond of pigs. Dogs look up to us. Cats look down on us. Pigs treat us as equals." — Winston Churchill

"'Tell Suzie she's a lucky cat.' Have sexier words ever been spoken?" — Ally Carter

"There is, incidentally, no way of talking about cats that enables one to come off as a sane person." — Dan Greenberg

"No matter how much the cats fight, there always seem to be plenty of kittens." — Abraham Lincoln

"Dogs own space and cats own time." — Nicola Griffith, *Hild*

"A woman hath nine lives like a cat." — John Heywood

"A kitten is the delight of a household. All day long a comedy is played out by an incomparable actor." — Champfleury, *The Cat, Past and Present*

"Cats are smarter than dogs. You can't get eight cats to pull a sled through snow." — Jeff Valdez

"If only cats grew into kittens." — Robert A. M. Ster

"Cats have been all over the Internet for many years. This makes total sense, as they seem to spend half their lives trying to stand and sit on the keyboards of our laptops." — Tom Cox, *The Good, The Bad, and the Furry*

"Dogs are always going to come up short if you insist on defining them as a weird kind of cat." — Peter Watts, *Echopraxia*

"The world would probably be better if people were put in carriers and cats roamed free." — Mary Matthews, *Splendid Summer*

"If the grass looked greener on my side of the fence, it was because my cats kept peeing near it." — Sheldon L. Adler

"Don't judge a cat by its coat." — Magdalena VandenBerg

"Dogs have owners. Cats have staff." — Unknown

"As anyone who has ever been around a cat for any length of time well knows, cats have enormous patience with the limitations of the humankind." — Cleveland Armory

"There's no need for a piece of sculpture in a home that has a cat." — Wesley Bates

"A cat is the only domestic animal I know who toilet trains itself and does a damn impressive job of it." — Joseph Epstein

"I'm trying to translate what my cat says and put it in a book, but how many homonyms are there for meow?" — Jarod Kintz

"Some people say that cats are sneaky, evil, and cruel. True, and they have many other fine qualities as well." — Missy Dizick

"It's really the cat's house—we just pay the mortgage." — Author Unknown

"Cats never strike a pose that isn't photogenic." — Lilian Jackson Braun

Cat Lover in Focus: Elizabeth Taylor

British-American actress Elizabeth Taylor dominated cinema, winning the Academy Award for *BUtterfield 8* (1960). Taylor was also a known cat lady.

Taylor took on several roles associated with cats throughout her career. For instance, she starred in the film adaptation of Tennessee Williams's *Cat on a Hot Tin Roof* in 1958. which, without featuring an actual kitty, took its title from the characters' cat-like fickleness of both loving the heat of a hot roof but also realizing that staying there is unsustainable.

Taylor's dazzling portrayal of Cleopatra, the Ancient Egyptian pharaoh whose culture worshipped cats, lives on today: many women flaunt Taylor's "cat's eye" makeup.

Offscreen, Elizabeth Taylor was often photographed with the many cats she owned or cherished. Taylor had an abiding love for Siamese cats in particular.

Taylor loved Siamese cats so much she gave her good friend American actor James Dean a pet Siamese she named "Marcus" to keep him company. You can see Dean with Marcus in this photograph:

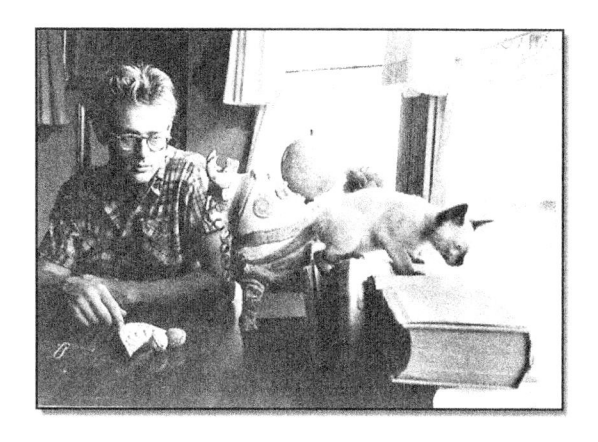

Since Taylor was known for her unusually beautiful eyes, which appeared to be purple, perhaps she found a kinship with this blue-eyed breed.

Taylor treated her cats with the reverence and love of children. She famously wrote a letter to her cat Cassius, who went missing during a film shoot. You can read it on the next page.

"Letter to my Lovely Lost Cat"

I see you, my beauty boy, in the reflection of those shining black-brown rocks ahead of me. I see the green o'thy eyes in every rained, sweated leaf shaking in my eyes.

I remember the sweet smell of your fur against my neck when I was deeply in trouble and how, somehow you made it better—you knew! You knew always when I hurt and you made comfort for me, as I did once for you when you were a broken kitten.

Anyway, I love you Cassius—and thank you for your beauty.

Please come back!

Acknowledgments

Thank you to my father for relenting and agreeing to let our family adopt two cats when I was young, and then later to allow a stray into our home and hearts. Thank you to everyone who has encouraged my love of cats. Thank you to all the cats who have healed me over the years, and thank you to my current cats for supporting me with comfort and love during hard times.

—Sarah S. Davis, September 2019

About the Author

Sarah S. Davis is a freelance writer, editor, and book content and marketing strategist based in the Philadelphia area. Sarah's writing about books has appeared on Kirkus Reviews, where she also served as a copywriter and production editor, as well as Book Riot, Electric Literature, Psych Central, EBSCOHost, BookRags, and many more. In 2014, Sarah started Broke by Books, a book blog whose guiding mission is to spread a contagious love for reading and help grow an inspired, engaged, and fearless reading life. She has published numerous books, including *A Reader's Library of Book Quotes, Brave Brain,* and *How to Write a Book Review.*

Sarah holds a BA in English from the University of Pennsylvania, a Master of Library and Information Science from Clarion University, and a Master of Fine Arts in Writing for Children and Young Adults from Vermont College of Fine Arts.

When she isn't reading or writing, Sarah enjoys leaning into cat lady spinsterhood, illustrating, reading tarot, and seeing as many films as she can.

Printed in Great Britain
by Amazon